What is Politics? Why Should we Care? And other Big Questions

Michael Rosen & Annemarie Young

WAYLAND
www.waylandbooks.co.uk

For Emma, Elsie and Emile (M.R.)
For Ben, introduced to politics at an early age! (A.Y.)

First published in Great Britain in 2019 by Wayland
Michael Rosen and Annemarie Young have asserted their rights to be identified as the Authors of this Work.
Text Copyright © Michael Rosen and Annemarie Young, 2019
Contributor text Copyright: James Graham's text pp18-19 © James Graham, 2019; Michelle Dorrell's text pp28-29
© Michelle Dorrell, 2019; Nimko Ali's text pp36-37 © Nimko Ali, 2019; Sir Stephen O'Brien's text pp40-41
© Sir Stephen O'Brien, 2019

Editor: Nicola Edwards
Design: Rocket Design (East Anglia) Ltd
Artwork by Oli Frape
ISBN 978 1 5263 0907 5 (hb) 978 1 5263 0906 8 (pb)
10 9 8 7 6 5 4 3 2 1

Wayland, an imprint of
Hachette Children's Group
Part of Hodder and Stoughton
Carmelite House
50 Victoria Embankment
London EC4Y 0DZ

An Hachette UK Company
www.hachette.co.uk
www.hachettechildrens.co.uk

Printed and bound in Dubai

We would like to thank: Nimko Ali, Michelle Dorrell, James Graham and Sir Stephen O'Brien for sharing their
experiences with us. All those who have contributed to the book in some way. Anthony Robinson, for his insightful
and useful comments on early drafts of the text.
And a big thank you to our excellent editor, Nicola Edwards, for her invaluable input, as always.

Picture acknowledgements:
Alamy: Mark Kerrison 42t. Anthony Robinson: Back cover (r); 9. Courtesy of Goldsmiths, University of London:
Back cover (l); 9. Courtesy of Sir Stephen O'Brien: 5b, 40. Febian Awondatu: 5cb, 28. Getty Images: Loop Images
15bl; Francis Miller/Time Life Pictures 34b; Gail Orenstein/Nur Photo 6b; Roberto Schmidt/AFP 22b; Jack Taylor
38b; Topical Press Agency 31c; Ann Ward/Mirrorpix 33c. Shutterstock: Bakounine 26tr; Evan El-Amin 24br; Kevin
J Frost 11c; Olga Kashubin 16b; a katz 30bl; Alexandros Michailidis 20b; Liv Oeian 27t; pseudolongino 32cl; lev
radin 24bl; Joseph Sohm 10b; Greg-Ward 45c. Sandra Freij: 5c, 36. Steve Tanner: 5t, 18.

J320.

JAN '20

JO

Renfrewshire
Council

The library is always open at
renfrewshirelibraries.co.uk

Visit now for
homework help
and free
eBooks.

We are the Skoobs and we love the library!

Phone: 0300 300 1188
Email: libraries@renfrewshire.gov.uk

Contents

What is this book about?

You might wonder 'What has politics got to do with me? Politics is about politicians, isn't it, and I can't vote until I'm 18, so why would I be interested?' But politicians and voting are only one aspect of politics. The broadest definition of politics is that it's about the use of power in all situations – from personal relationships all the way to state power. And because it's all around us it's impossible to walk away from it. This is why we think it's important to understand what politics is all about.

Politics is everywhere

We are all involved daily in situations and decisions that are political in some sense. What are these situations and how do we make decisions? How can we think about situations in a way that will help us to make the best decisions? Can we make any difference to the big, global questions?

This book is not going to tell you what to think. We give you information and raise many questions. Our aim is to get you to think for yourselves about these questions.

We think it's important that everyone should think about and talk about life's big questions, and never just accept what they are told. This doesn't mean that you can't continue to hold the ideas or values that you had, but if you do, you'll know that those values are your own and not just an unthinking acceptance of someone else's ideas. This applies as much to politics in all its senses as it does to other beliefs and ideas.

How does the book work?

We'll introduce you to different aspects of politics, examining such questions as: what is politics and what forms does it take? Can you be non-political? What is political power? How do political systems differ around the world? Does language have political influence? What difference can political action make? Why does politics cause such division and disagreement? And we'll show you how people have responded to situations and events in history.

Of course, we couldn't possibly fit into this one book all the information you need in order to answer all the questions we raise. Instead, we provide you with information about some of the key ideas and make suggestions for you to follow up.

We'll also ask you to think about how some of the issues relate to your life and your political ideas, and give you the opportunity to set up your own discussions to find out what other people think.

The people in the book

We'll tell you about ourselves, and how we developed our own ideas and values. You will be able to read quotes from speeches Riz Ahmed and Greta Thunberg made to the UK Parliament on issues they felt passionately about. You will also hear from four people involved in politics in different ways – Nimko Ali, Michelle Dorrell, James Graham and Sir Stephen O'Brien – who'll discuss their own experiences and thoughts on the subject. In addition there will be quotes from other people spread through the book.

At the end

We'll ask you to reflect on what you've read, and on the discussions you've had while reading the book. We'll ask you:

- Did any of these ideas surprise you? If yes, why?

- What points and values best reflect your own ideas?

- Did you change your mind about anything?

James Graham

Nimko Ali

Michelle Dorrell

"What people are looking for is a message that they belong, that they're part of something, that they are seen and heard, that they are valued."

Riz Ahmed, speaking to the UK Parliament in 2017 on why it's important that everyone should be represented in politics.

Sir Stephen O'Brien

What is politics?

As we've said, the broadest definition of politics is that it's about the use of power in all situations – from personal relationships to state power. Any use of power that influences behaviour is political. Let's look at some examples of situations that are political, even if they don't immediately appear to be.

People and politics

There might be concerns about people parking too close to the entrance of your school, making it dangerous for the children coming in. Or there might be a local bully who is making people feel unsafe in their homes. On a larger scale, the way that vulnerable people – for example, children or adults with particular needs – are categorised and treated in our society and through our laws, is political. And, of course, nationally, there are the discussions in Parliament about whether to invade a sovereign state, like Iraq.

Politics as a process

Politics is the process of making decisions – including the establishment of rules and laws – as they apply to a grouping of people in society, whether it's a small group or an entire country. This process is usually not straightforward, because people will always have differing views on the issues and disagree about how they should be resolved. Who should have a say? How should decisions be made? Do the different groupings agree to compromise, or does the winning group have it all their way? The issue of Brexit in the UK shows just how difficult it can be, while the Good Friday agreement of 1998 regarding Northern Ireland, demonstrates how two sides can come to an agreement, even after years of conflict.

Various levels

You could think of life as being like a building with different floors. In the same way, we could say that we live politics at different levels. One level might be about joining campaigns or demonstrations.

Supporters and opponents of Brexit demonstrate outside the Houses of Parliament in 2019.

Another level could be discussing elections and deciding how to vote. Another might be listening to our parents and others talking about some of the big decisions they've made, for example moving countries, or how they resolved a serious difficulty. Did they look for help from a Member of Parliament (MP)? A local councillor? A lawyer?

Yet another level might be the one that looks the least political: how and why we relate to each other. For example, do we dismiss other people because they're not like us (colour, age, background)? Do we tend to try to control other people? Or do others control us? Or do we try to find ways to work together and co-operate to solve problems?

HOW CAN THE PERSONAL BE POLITICAL?

Here are some examples.

Homosexuality
Formerly in the UK, homosexuality – personal sexual relationships between two people of the same sex – was a criminal act, and people were imprisoned for their personal choices. This is still the case in a number of countries around the world.

More recently, campaigns have resulted in civil partnerships and gay marriage being made legal.

Laws against harassment and racism
Until recent years, it was not against the law, for example, for people to be bullied or harassed in the workplace, or for someone to discriminate against a person because of their skin colour. Now there are laws protecting a person's right to be free from racial or sexual harassment.

And what about personal taste, such as the amount of salt or sugar in processed food? When you cook something yourself, you decide how much salt or sugar to use, but when you buy processed food, it's been decided. This became a political issue, resulting in legislation to regulate limits.

My experience

Michael Rosen

Michael Rosen is a writer for adults and children, a broadcaster and Professor of Children's Literature at Goldsmiths, University of London.

⚡ I've always been political

All my life, I've been someone people describe as 'political'. As a child, I was taken to meetings and on demonstrations. I can remember being ten years old with my parents and protesting about Britain being part of several armies that invaded Egypt. When I was a teenager, I joined marches that protested about Britain having nuclear bombs, and I protested about Apartheid in South Africa.

We've talked about our life being a bit like a building. In buildings, the floors connect to each other with staircases and lifts. This view of our lives as being on different levels also relates to how our levels connect to each other.

⚡ The arts make connections

I've spent a lot of my life writing books, going to the movies and the theatre, listening to music, going to art galleries. Do you know Charles Dickens's book *A Christmas Carol*? It tells the story of a mean old man, Scrooge, and how he comes to see that his life and his politics (on several levels at the same time) are wrong.

His personal un-loving self (at one level) is connected to how he treats the man who works for him (another level), which is in turn connected to his attitude to how society as a whole should treat poor people (yet another level).

Do you know Shakespeare's *Romeo and Juliet*? The play connects the levels between two people's love for each other, with the social circumstances of two families who hate each other, and how the families' need for wealth and status interferes with the young people's love.

I spend a lot of my life writing, broadcasting and teaching — thinking about these connections. Sometimes this leads me to being political in the obvious sense of going on demonstrations and speaking at them (see pages 42-43). At other times, it's trying to think about fair and just ways to interact with the people I meet, know and live with.

> "All my life, I've been someone people describe as 'political'."

My experience

Annemarie Young

Annemarie Young was a publisher and now writes stories and information books for young people.

☀ What did I care about?

Fairness

From an early age I was sensitive to the notion of fairness. My family were immigrants and I could see how, in the South Australian community where I grew up, migrants were often treated differently from those born in the country.

I remember experiencing dislike and 'othering' because of my parents' background. When I was about four, an older boy called me names and threw a small rock at me, which hit me on the head – I was shocked and frightened.

Racism

As I grew older, I noticed that others who were different were also discriminated against. This included Aboriginal people – the original inhabitants of Australia – who suffered even more from racism, and weren't all granted the right to vote or full Australian citizenship until 1967!

Political action

By my mid-teens, I realised that my views on fairness were political. At the time, Australia was involved in the Vietnam war, and the Apartheid regime in South Africa was entrenched. I decided to take action by campaigning against both these situations, as well as for Aboriginal rights.

Feminism, power and language

At a young age the status of women in society was important to me. I was conscious that women and girls were considered less able, and had fewer choices than men and boys.

I hated the way that 'man' was used to refer to everyone, and 'he' was used as if it included women and girls: for example, 'mankind' rather than 'humankind' and "Ask any doctor and he'll tell you …". This usage made women and girls invisible, and the male perspective more important. Along with others, I started campaigning to make singular 'they' acceptable and to find more inclusive language. Thanks to these campaigns, singular 'they' and other inclusive use of language is now common.

> "my views on fairness were political"

What forms does politics take?

'Political forms' are the kinds of organisations or systems that exist in a particular society to run that society. The idea of everyone above a certain age having the vote is a political form. The idea of having a group of generals running a country is a political form.

What follows from this is that we can discuss which political forms are best, or how they might be changed, abolished or reformed. How this might happen is, of course, very political. Let's look at an example.

Choosing a government

In the UK, we vote for and elect MPs in our locality. The party that has the most MPs gets to form the government, which is made up of the Prime Minister, who chooses her or his ministers, some of whom are in a special committee called the Cabinet.

This is one form of democracy. In the USA and France, people vote for a President, as well as voting for Representatives in their localities. They also vote for Senators who together make up a Second Chamber which has a final say in some of the law-making.

Voting at a polling station in the USA.

We'll talk more about voting systems around the world later in the book (see pages 22-23).

The UK system uses 'first past the post' to determine who gets into power. This means that one party might get millions of votes but only a handful of MPs because of the number of voters in their constituencies. Another party may get many fewer votes but more MPs. You might think another system would be more fair, such as 'proportional representation' – whoever gets the most votes gets the most MPs – or the preferential voting system, where you're able to vote for the candidates in your order of preference.

Political expression

Let's say you believe the system needs to be changed. What can you do about it?

Here are some of the ways:

Political parties
Some political parties, like the Conservative Party in Britain, are very old. Others, for

example, 'En Marche' in France, are very new. If you are under 18, you may well find that these political parties have sections that young people can join. Political parties usually have a core set of values. The idea is for the parties to work out policies on how to run the country in ways that put these values into practice if they are elected to govern.

Campaign groups
Usually these groups campaign on single issues – for example on conservation, child poverty, blood sports – or very local issues, like trying to save a local hospital from closing.

Charities
Some charities are strictly speaking not 'political' but collect money and campaign to get things done in areas where people feel that governments aren't doing, or can't do, enough: for example, saving wildlife, improving literacy.

THINK ABOUT

Some people prefer to express their politics through supporting charities, as they feel it's a practical way to help improve things. Others think that charities don't change anything, because governments are happy for charities to help clean up the mess that governments and society leaves.

What do you think? You could debate this question with other people.

Trade unions
Trade unions enable people in work to meet up and come to decisions about what to do about the conditions of work and people's pay.

Informal groups
When political events move fast – war, famine, refugees – campaigners, charities and informal organisations (as with the 'gilets jaunes' (yellow vests) in France) often respond with demonstrations, fund-raising, new organisations for that particular event, and so on.

An Extinction Rebellion protest march. This international movement says it uses "non-violent direct action to persuade governments to act on the Climate and Ecological Emergency".

Representative organisations
There are also many organisations which represent say, business interests, or doctors, or English teachers, footballers – almost any walk of life. These organisations meet to discuss the interests of the people in that field of work and, if they think their profession or line of work or interest, needs something from government or from the public at large, they campaign, and 'lobby'. This means going to the government and asking for more funding or for a change in policy.

Is it possible to have no politics? Can you be non-political?

The first question to ask might be 'What makes something political?' The answer is that anything that engages in either changing or supporting the 'status quo' (the present situation) can be called political. On this definition you can see that it's not really possible to have 'no politics'.

THINK ABOUT

How would you describe the status quo in the country you live in?

To answer that, you might want to think about:

- How the country is governed.

- How the government is chosen.

- How the economy is run – everything to do with business: the financing, making, distributing and selling of the things and services we need.

- How you get the services that are not directly part of business – like schools, health care, children's services, and all the work that charities do.

- The justice system: police, courts, prisons, judges and lawyers.

- The media: newspapers, TV, radio, and the internet, social media.

- The arts: painting, novels, plays, dance, singing, ceramics, architecture, poetry and so on.

Descriptions and attitudes are political

The descriptions you come up with are political, and your attitude to them is political. For example, you might be 100 per cent in favour of the whole set-up in your country, the whole status quo. Or, you might be in favour of some parts of it and want to change some others. Whatever your attitude, it is political.

Is it possible to be non-political?

When someone says they aren't political, they mostly mean that they don't support a political party, or that they don't know enough about national politics, and don't think it matters to them. Or perhaps, they can't see how they can make a difference because they are just individuals.

But most people, to some degree, care about what happens in their community, and they have views and opinions about local issues (for example local schools and hospitals and other amenities), and some national institutions. The National Health Service (NHS) is a good example of this in the UK.

If, for example, you break your leg, an ambulance will collect you and take you to hospital, and you won't have to pay for any of the care you will get – including hospitalisation, surgery and drugs.

The NHS is political because the government is responsible for it, and it's paid for by the government through general taxes. Compare this with the situation in countries such as the United States, which doesn't have a universal healthcare system, and where a significant number of people have difficulty accessing health care because of the costs involved.

THINK ABOUT

THE NATIONAL HEALTH SERVICE

- Do you think the NHS should continue with its founding principles to be 'comprehensive, universal and free at the point of delivery'? Why or why not?

- Some people think more money should go into the NHS via a special tax. Other people think more and more of the NHS should be in the hands of private companies. What do you think?

IS IT POSSIBLE TO HAVE A SOCIETY WITH NO POLITICAL SYSTEM?

When an old political system is overthrown, the chaos that ensues is not sustainable – human beings are pack animals, and groups always organise themselves in some way. So something always fills the vacuum left by the previous power. Here are some examples to find out more about.

- The Reign of Terror in France during the French Revolution (1789–1799) – during which time there were 17,000 official death sentences.

- Russia in the period just after the 1917 Revolution.

- Iraq since the removal of Saddam Hussein by the Coalition Forces (2003).

- Libya since the civil war and military intervention (2011).

What is political power?

Three branches

In most modern democracies, power is divided between three branches of government: executive, legislature and judiciary. The reason for having three separate branches is so that there are what are called 'checks and balances', meaning that no one can have too much power, and the 'rule of law' (which places limits on the power of government, institutions and business) can be safeguarded.

The separations of power apply in different ways in different countries. In the UK, Parliament is the **legislative** branch of government. There are two 'chambers', the fully elected House of Commons (HoC), and the partially elected House of Lords (HoL). Laws start off as 'Bills' which are voted on at different 'readings' just as you might do at school where a teacher asks a class to discuss and then vote on something.

If both houses of parliament vote for the Bill (first reading in HoC, second reading HoL, third reading back to HoC) the Bill goes to the monarch to sign and the Bill becomes an Act – that is, it becomes a law.

The **executive** consists of the Prime Minister and Cabinet, and local branches of government. They carry out the business of government, implementing ('executing') the Bills agreed by Parliament.

The **judiciary** is made up of the court system. In the UK, it's the members of the judiciary who decide how to interpret the laws. The Supreme Court – the highest court in the country – is where decisions are taken in cases where there are disagreements and people have appealed against decisions made in the lower courts. Judges are appointed and approved by panels of experts outside the judiciary, to try to ensure they are impartial.

In the UK there is a Scottish Assembly, a Welsh Assembly, and a government in Northern Ireland called Stormont (suspended in 2017 over policy disagreements). These parliaments and governments have powers over some of the things that go on in those parts of the UK.

Does this explain all the power in the country?

No. There are other kinds of local government, called councils – some with different kinds of mayor, where we elect people for different kinds of local authority. These too have some power over what goes on in a locality. There is also the question of who owns what: land, businesses and resources, as well as the power of the relatively ungoverned internet. All these examples come with power attached.

Does that explain all the power in the country? No. There are some parts of society which have power over our lives but are not part of government. The most obvious of these is business.

The Debating Chamber of the Welsh Assembly building in Cardiff, opened in 2006.

"Politics hates a vacuum.
If it isn't filled with hope,
someone will fill it
with fear."

Naomi Klein, author and activist

Business and other institutions

Business is one word to describe all the different firms, companies, industries, offices, institutions and organisations which finance, make, distribute and sell what we need and use. A few of the institutions – like education and the health service – are run by the government. Most are run by business people.

Some businesses are run and owned by a group of people at the top of the company. Some are owned by shareholders – that's people who have bought (or been given) shares in a company. This is a way of lending money to a company. You might do this in the hope that these shares will become more valuable. That would happen if the company was able to sell its goods or services at a profit – which means the company makes more money than it spends. A company spends money on things like rent, buying what it needs to make the goods or sell the services, and wages and salaries for the people it employs.

All this tells you that this world of business and institutions involves all of the people in the country. This is because we are buying the goods and services, or because we are employed, or because we are the people in charge. We are also involved if we are saving money in a bank or for a pension (money you get when you retire). That's because the people looking after your savings invest your money in different ways, including buying shares in companies, in order to get a financial return.

This photo shows the Central Business District in Sydney, Australia – a concentration of businesses in one area.

Not part of government

Now here's a big but: most of this way of running all that employment (millions of employees) and making or delivering all these goods and services is not part of government. There are laws that govern what they can and can't do, but this system of delivering what we want and need is not run by elected officials; this means they are very powerful but we have no way of holding them to account if they follow these laws. Another powerful area outside of government is the media.

The media

We hear a good deal about politics through the print press (newspapers, magazines, journals etc) and other media: television, radio, the internet. Does the media provide another means of political power?

The mass media in Britain are mostly privately owned, apart from the BBC. Other countries have different set-ups.

A big question for all countries is: who owns and controls the media? Are there a number of different owners with different political allegiances? Or is most of it controlled by a small number of people or groups?

Do the media control how a topic is 'framed'? Think about advertising and promotions in the media, for example, the images we are shown of war zones, gambling, alcohol, political broadcasts. Think about Brexit, Extinction Rebellion, immigrants and refugees.

Censorship, whistle blowers and journalists in danger

In some countries there is overt censorship of the media, for example: Turkey (hundreds of journalists arrested), Saudi Arabia (women's rights defenders), Hungary (new laws restricting freedom of expression).

In other places, journalists who criticise the government or investigate other powerful entities are silenced by being threatened or imprisoned, and in some instances even killed. Sometimes, shadowy groups carry out 'extra-judicial' (outside the law) killings of investigative journalists or whistle blowers (people who call out wrongdoing from inside an organisation). There are many examples from South America, and investigative journalists have been threatened and beaten, and even killed in countries like the US. Israel kidnapped and subsequently imprisoned a nuclear technician, Mordechai Vanunu, for whistle blowing – revealing information about Israel's secret nuclear weapons programme.

The whole set-up

Of course, politics can also be about the whole set-up: for example, do you think all this is a fair, just and sensible way to run things, or do you think it should be reformed, or completely changed?

When people talk about, say, the economic crisis of 2008, or inequality, or poverty, they are often asking questions about the whole set-up.

And remember that being in favour of the status quo is as political as not being in favour of it (see page 12).

My experience

James Graham

James Graham is a playwright and screenwriter who likes to dramatise political stories, from the European Referendum in the TV drama *Brexit: The Uncivil War*, to how parliament works in the play *This House*. For the general election in 2015 he wrote *The Vote* which was a play staged and broadcast live on television during the last 90 minutes of polling. He has won an Olivier Award for his stage work, and a Royal Television Society Award for the screen.

⚡ The who and where of politics

When I'm writing a play or a film script, one of the first things I have to decide is *who* should be a character, and *where* it should be set.

Who and *where* can be issues when we think about politics too. That's because, with politics, we often think about *other people*. A separate group called 'politicians'.

But the word 'democracy' comes from the joining together of the Greek word *demos*, meaning 'common people', and *kratos*, meaning power or strength. So politics is actually meant to be about the strength of normal people, coming together.

⚡ Who?

Emmeline Pankhurst, at the end of the nineteenth century, decided she wanted to be part of the *who* in politics. At the time, women weren't allowed to vote. Her brave campaigning with the suffragettes changed this in 1918. She wrote herself and other women into the cast of characters.

Many years later, someone who excited me enough to write a play about them was a working-class London man called David Sutch, who decided to invent the character of a fictional aristocrat called Screaming Lord Sutch. He stood in elections playing this part for over 30 years with jokey policies such as abolishing January and February "because they're too cold", and shortening the queue at the job centre by "making people stand closer together". But the serious point he was trying to make was that if he can run for parliament, anyone can. Politics isn't just about the right to vote, but the right to be voted *for*.

✳ And what about where?

We often think politics is set in the Houses of Parliament. Or the White House. Very old, grand buildings that feel far away. But one of the reasons why I became interested in politics when I was young was because of where I grew up: a small mining village in Nottinghamshire. That's because my village was the scene of some angry clashes about the closing of the coal mines by the government.

During a year-long dispute in 1984 called the Miners' Strike, some of the coal miners decided to strike in protest, but others wanted to keep working. Picket lines were formed, where you had to pick a side. The violent scenes that erupted left two impressions on me. Firstly, to try and appreciate *both sides*, because political arguments can sometimes make us very unsympathetic to other people's points of view. Secondly, that things are not always black and white, right or wrong. It's often more complicated, and people are more complicated, than just Striking or Not Striking, or voting Leave or voting Remain.

One of my favourite political figures is Martin Luther King. He wasn't a politician, but he fought for the civil rights of African Americans in the 1960s, using civil, kind and compassionate methods, believing it was better to encourage understanding within his opponents, rather than inciting their antagonism.

✳ Deciding what to do

A favourite quote, which isn't explicitly political, comes from James Lovell, an American astronaut, who said that America got to the Moon first because "we just decided to go".

Equal rights Emmeline Pankhurst just decided that women should have the vote. Martin Luther King, Jr decided that black Americans deserved the same rights as whites.

Disease Smallpox was a deadly virus that killed hundreds of thousands of people. But a vaccine was invented, and by 1977, the last ever person was diagnosed with smallpox, making it the first virus to be extinguished from the planet.

Poverty After a pledge from The World Bank, poverty is being reduced too. Since the year 2000, levels of global poverty have been reduced by half.

Sport The British Olympics team used to come really low down in the medals table. In the 1990s, both Conservative and Labour governments set a target to change this, with investment in sports for young people. Two decades later, Great Britain came third in the medals table in London 2012, beating China, one of their highest ever positions. This was a political decision.

That's why politics should also be about optimism, as well as anger. It is possible for all sorts of people, from all sorts of places, to come together and make a difference.

" ... politics should also be about optimism, as well as anger."

Does language have political influence?

At the heart of all talking and writing is choice. Think about asking someone to leave the room. Do you say: "Excuse me, would you please leave the room?" Or "Clear off!" Or what?

What guides you in this choice? One factor is how you think of the person you're talking to. Another might be the effect you might have. This is mainly to do with your status or power in relation to the other person. Will you be talking 'up', 'down' or on equal terms to the person?

Differences in power between people is political.

Political language

Now let's look at some of the ways people in politics use language.

Dehumanising

Historically, people have often referred to those they oppose in ways that take away their human qualities. One way is to give individuals or groups animal names. In Nazi Germany, Jews were called vermin by the authorities. Vermin had to be got rid of. They were. This is one of the most extreme ways language can be political.

Boris Johnson

In 2018 the politician Boris Johnson (below left) wrote an article in a national newspaper where he described some Muslim women as looking like letter-boxes. Does it dehumanise to compare a woman's appearance to a letter-box? Was he talking 'down' or 'up' or as an equal?

Legitimating

This is the use of language in such a way that it *appears to be* right. Here's an example.

You have to give a speech about people leaving their lights on all night. You can begin your speech in different ways:

1. "We hate it, don't we?"
2. "I have a statistic showing that 45 per cent of us leave our lights on all night."
3. "The truth is, people leave their lights on all night."
4. "It's been said that people are leaving their lights on all night."

Which one do you choose and why? Do you have another way to begin?

(1) The speaker is creating a divide between 'us' – good, and 'them' – bad.
(2) Employs statistics and uses the inclusive 'us.' Is the statistic true or fair?
(3) Tells us it's the 'truth'. Who says?
(4) Uses the passive: 'It's been said...' Who by? Where? This represents the voice of some unknown authority.

Those are four different ways to 'legitimate' what is said, all in order to convince you that there's a problem.

Point of view

Whose point of view do you use? The decision is political. In this fictional example, imagine that the Ruritanians and Tombolans, living in the same country, are in conflict. The Ruritanians say that the Tombolans spend all their time on the street and are wearing out the pavements. The Tombolans say that their houses are too small to stay home. You've got a speech to give about this. Do you tell the story as a Ruritanian problem, or as a Tombolan one? Do you tell both sides of the story? Do you spend more time on one point of view rather than on the other?

Terms of reference

You're a government representative and you have to talk about this Ruritanian-Tombolan conflict. Do you mention the fact that the Ruritanians invaded Tombola? Which is fairer – to mention it or not to mention it?

Statistics

Statistics depend on what question is being answered, and how the figures have been calculated. People often use statistics to make claims without explaining how they have been calculated.

Here's an example of how numbers can make something sound like good news when it might be quite different: A politician announces: 'Now more and more Tombolans are in work. Hurrah!'

But here's the background information: Ten years ago, most Tombolans worked 40 hours a week for £10.00 an hour (£400.00 per week). There was a crisis and most Tombolans lost their jobs. Now those Tombolans are in work again, but they're working only one hour per week, earning £10.00 per week.

Is this good news for the Tombolans?

THINK ABOUT

Look at any dispute past or present and see if you can find the point of view. Can you see how this is political? What would the dispute look like from the other side's point of view?

How do political systems vary around the world?

Countries have many different political systems. Here are some of the variations:

A country can have a president who has hardly any power, or one who has enormous power. The president can be chosen by popular vote, separately from the election of members for a congress or parliament. And sometimes, the majority in a congress or assembly might not belong to the president's party.

Many countries have a second chamber whose members review the laws that are passed. Usually, this second chamber is fully elected, but not in the UK (the House of Lords). In other countries, like the US, this second chamber is called the Senate.

As a voter, you might decide to vote for different parties. For example, you might vote one way for your Representative (or Member of Parliament); for another party when you vote for the president, and another party when you vote for the senator.

In most, but not all, countries you can vote from a certain age. In Australia, voting is compulsory.

The electoral college system in the United States

In this system, areas vote to choose an 'electoral college' – this is the group of people who will then vote for the president on their behalf. Whichever party wins the most votes in that area, wins the whole college. The losing party in that area gets no votes at all. This is called a 'winner-takes-all' system. Each of the colleges' pre-arranged totals are added together to see which of the presidential candidates is the winner.

India's 2019 general election involved 900 million voters. Special arrangements had to be made to allow people in remote areas, including mountains and dense forests, to vote.

Different ways of deciding who wins an election

In France, you vote locally. If the most popular candidate wins over 50 per cent of the votes, and from at least 25 per cent of the people eligible to vote, that person becomes the Representative, or the Deputy. If this does not happen, there's a second round. This time, the only people who can stand are those who won at least 12.5 per cent of the votes of eligible voters. The person who wins the most votes on this second round, wins.

Some countries run elections according to a system called a 'single transferable vote',

where you vote for your first and your second choice.

Then there are different ways of counting: one way is to first count all the first votes in your locality. If one candidate wins an outright majority (50+ per cent of votes), that person wins. If not, they add the second votes for the candidates and get a winner that way.

With some systems, you don't vote in a locality, but for a party. Each party has a long list of people it wants to be elected. The votes are totalled up. Percentage scores are worked out. These percentages are then reflected in the assembly/parliament.

Citizens' assemblies

A citizens' assembly is a group of people who are brought together to discuss issues and make recommendations. The people who take part are chosen to reflect the demographic makeup of the population (for example, in age, gender, ethnicity, location and social class).

One example: The Citizens' Assembly in the Republic of Ireland

This was set up in 2016 to consider several complex political questions, including abortion.

One of the members has written, "We wanted to take in all the information, help shape the debate and make solid recommendations that were representative of all our views at the end of a period of deep learning about the topics."

After hearing both pro- and anti-abortion views and taking advice from a panel of medical and legal professionals, the assembly

made its recommendations to parliament, calling for unrestricted access to abortion. There was widespread shock at this, but at the subsequent referendum on the subject in 2018, 66 per cent voted in favour of unrestricted abortion.

THINK ABOUT

Citizens' assemblies are being proposed for local concerns, such as transport in Cambridge, UK; regional issues, for example, how best to encourage investment into particular regions; and national issues, like what the country as a whole should do about climate change.

Find out more about citizens' assemblies. Do you think they could help to solve major issues, where other systems have failed? Why or why not?

Why should we care?

We've looked at how being 'non-political' in effect means supporting the status quo, whatever that is. It means not thinking about or questioning the current state of affairs. The effect of this – whether it's by not voting or by not taking part in local or national discussions and campaigns – is that we let other people take the decisions. Where does this lead?

Why vote?

Do the people who think of themselves as non-political and choose not to vote have any effect on who gets into power? If these people don't vote, it means that a smaller percentage of the population makes the decision about who governs the country. Does this matter?

For example, in the 2016 US election, 58.1 per cent of eligible voters voted in the elections, and approximately one quarter of them voted for Donald Trump. His Democratic rival, Hillary Clinton, received a higher percentage of the 'popular' vote (that is, in relation to the total number of people who voted), but because of the

electoral college system (see page 22), he won and became president. So, three quarters of the electorate did not vote for him. How does this sound to you? And what difference might the 41.9 per cent of eligible voters who didn't vote have made to the result?

Why voting matters

The 2016 Brexit Referendum in the UK provides another example of why voting matters. The overall result was that 52 per cent of those who voted were in favour of leaving the EU, with 48 per cent voting to remain. Now look at the breakdown of voters in terms of how people in different age groups voted. Of the 72 per cent of

Donald Trump (above left) greets supporters after beating Hillary Clinton (above right) in the 2016 election to become the 45th president of the United States.

the electorate who turned out to vote, over 70 per cent of the 18- to 24-year-olds who voted, backed Remain, with just under 30 per cent backing Leave. In contrast, only 40 per cent of those aged 65 and over supported Remain, while 60 per cent supported Leave.

Fewer people turned out to vote in areas with a younger population and, before the actual vote, only half of those aged 18 to 24 said they were certain they would vote, compared with two thirds of those over 65. Had the turnout of young people been similar to that of people over 65, the result could have been quite different.

> "Instead of feeling dejected, I think this result has led many young people to become more determined to have their say."

Phoebe Warneford-Thomson, aged 18, speaking to a reporter from The Guardian *in 2016*

Some people think they don't count and can't make a difference

Does poverty or class make a difference to whether or not people feel they can become politically engaged? The rapper

and social commentator Darren McGarvey (who raps as Loki) has written in his book, *Poverty Safari,* that apathy (a lack of interest or concern) in many communities might be a result of people believing that different rules apply to them compared with those who are better off. And this belief leads them to think that the system is rigged against them and that all attempts to challenge it are pointless; that the decisions that affect their lives are taken by people elsewhere who deliberately try to exclude them from the decision making. What do you think?

> "... there are so many people in communities that turn on their televisions or pick up their newspapers and they don't see their authentic selves reflected or depicted."

Darren McGarvey, interviewed in The Observer *in 2018*

On the next pages you can read what the actor, rapper and activist Riz Ahmed said about the need for politics to represent everyone, and about the actions of young climate activist Greta Thunberg.

Riz Ahmed

Riz Ahmed (right) is an Emmy-award-winning actor, rapper and activist. He gave the annual Channel 4 Diversity Speech to the House of Commons in Britain in 2017. In his speech he talked about the importance of representation in politics. You can listen to the whole speech on YouTube.

"I'm here to ask for your help in finding a new national story that embraces and empowers as many of us as possible rather than excluding us and alienating sections of the population."

"We're talking about representation, not diversity. Representation's not an added extra, it's not a frill, it's fundamental to what people expect from culture and from politics."

How can I possibly make a difference?

Many things have come together recently, leading people to think about how they might bring about change more quickly, outside the more traditional political forms.

Climate change, deforestation and the destruction of habitats, the effects of plastic pollution, and the serious health effects of air pollution, are all forcing people to think hard about our current priorities.

THINK ABOUT

Do you care about politics, or not? What about the people you know?

Do you/they still wonder what politics has to do with you/them?

If you think that politics has nothing to do with you, what do you think the consequences of thinking this way might be?

Greta Thunberg

Greta Thunberg is a student from Sweden. One Friday in August 2018, aged 15, she started a school strike (not going to school) for the climate outside the Swedish parliament building. She was on her own, carrying a banner that read '*skolstrejk för klimatet*' (school strike for climate) (above). She continued striking every Friday, and she was soon joined by others. The movement has now grown to over 70 countries and 700 locations. In one of her speeches she said, "No one is too small to make a difference."

The climate strike was inspired by students from the Parkland school in Florida, who walked out of classes in protest against the US gun laws they say enabled the massacre at their school. Greta was part of a group that wanted to do something similar to raise awareness about climate change, but the group couldn't agree on what to do. In the summer of 2018, after a terrible heatwave in northern Europe, and forest fires that ravaged parts of Sweden up to the Arctic, Greta decided to act alone.

This is what Greta told political leaders and billionaire entrepreneurs at the World Economic Forum meeting in Davos in 2019, "I don't want you to be hopeful. I want you to panic. I want you to feel the fear I feel every day. And then I want you to act."

"We children are not sacrificing our education and our childhood for you to tell us what you consider is politically possible in the society that you have created ... We children are doing this to wake the adults up. We children are doing this for you to put your differences aside and start acting as you would in a crisis. We children are doing this because we want our hopes and dreams back."

Greta Thunberg, speaking to the UK parliament in 2019

My experience

Michelle Dorrell

Michelle Dorrell grew up in Kent. She worked from the age of sixteen and held jobs in tele-sales and retail. She's now the Communications Officer for the Co-operative Schools Network, and a Refugee Mobile Education Charity called the School Bus Project.

☀ Waking up to politics

The Iraq war in 2003 started to wake me up to politics; before that I'd been politically apathetic. Then in 2011, returning from maternity leave, I was refused a change in working hours. I ended up quitting the job because I was too stressed to fight. Now, for the first time, I was an unemployed single mother with no income. After failing to find a new position, I found myself on Income Support – I had become one of those people the media portrayed as a failure and a scrounger.

I lost all my self-confidence and sense of self-worth.

☀ Broken promises

At one of the debates in the run-up to the general election in May 2015, David Cameron (who was the Prime Minister and leader of the Conservative Party) was asked if they were going to cut tax credits for working people on low incomes. I was by this time relying on tax credits to make ends meet. He said no. I believed him and voted Conservative. But after the Conservatives had won the election, the Chancellor of the Exchequer, George Osborne, announced they were going to cut tax credits.

One day I was watching 'Question Time' on TV and saw it was coming to my area the following week. I decided to go.

I submitted a question: "Pre-election, David Cameron promised not to cut tax credits, but that's the first thing to be cut. Why did you lie?". I wasn't one of those selected to ask their question, but the topic was discussed, and listening to the Cabinet minister Amber Rudd defending her party's actions made me very angry. Late in the filming she said, "the Conservative Party are bringing back the economic security of this country". From the pit of my stomach, a ball of words came to me and I started shouting: "I voted Conservative because I thought you were going to be the better chance for me and my children. You're about to cut tax credits after promising you wouldn't. I work hard to provide for my children, and you're going to take it away from me and them. I can hardly afford the rent and the bills I have to pay, and you're going to take more from me."

⁂ Becoming politically aware

This was a turning point. I'd only been getting my information from the *Sun*, the *Daily Mail*, the BBC and Sky. I started talking to people I'd never talked to before and realised my knowledge of politics was very limited. I decided to talk to every political party. Only two people responded: Heidi Allen of the Conservatives and John McDonnell of Labour.

I was invited to talk to them. I told Heidi Allen my story. She said she thought the Conservative Party still represented my sort of politics. I told her that her party's actions were causing knock-on consequences.

John McDonnell was very different. He didn't try to convince me of his politics. He wanted to listen to what I had to say. I went away feeling encouraged, useful and that I had something worth saying.

John McDonnell then invited me to a meeting of Momentum (a new political movement within the Labour Party). This was a big step. I listened to junior doctors, teachers, and others who are keeping our country going. And I suddenly understood how messed up our country was. This switched on something inside me.

I decided I couldn't just wait for someone else to say the things that need to be said – I felt I had to do it myself – and I joined the Labour Party. I'm now a candidate in the local elections.

⁂ Why should we care about politics?

Politics is about the society and community you want to live in. If you divide society and break it down, it leads to fear – which is on the rise – as well as pain and anxiety, because we see ourselves as individuals rather than as part of a whole.

What's been happening is 'divide and rule': the story is that it's the disabled person, the elderly, the migrant, the single mother, who are causing the problems, whereas we should be looking at those who are making the decisions that cause the underlying problems. That's what politics is all about, and that's why we should all care.

> "...we should be looking at those who are making the decisions that cause the underlying problems."

What difference can political action make?

We've talked about political parties and about charities (see page 11). Campaigns are another way to get involved in politics. They usually focus on one particular issue, for example, a proposal to close a hospital. In a situation like this a group of people against the closure try to get enough support locally and nationally to prevent it.

What methods do campaigns use?

Campaigners hold a meeting with as many people who care about the issue as possible. At the meeting, they have speakers who will explain what's being proposed and make suggestions as to what can be done. The meeting may elect a committee to take the campaign forward.

This committee may decide to do things like:

- Produce a leaflet explaining what's happening and what they see as the consequences of the closure.

- Hold a vigil at a time and place to gain maximum attention – perhaps outside the hospital.

- Collect signatures for a petition.

- Start up a website and use email and social media to spread information.

- Contact newspapers, TV and radio.

- Try to win support from local councillors, local MPs, famous local people, local trade unions, professional organisations and religious bodies.

- Contact other campaigns doing similar things elsewhere in the country.

In such campaigns, people generally try to think what kind of actions would be most effective and realistic, always bearing in mind that people are busy, at work, looking after children or otherwise preoccupied.

On the following pages, we'll look at some examples of how people have taken political action throughout history and the changes they brought about.

One of many marches over the years in Times Square, New York, protesting over police violence and the deaths of African Americans caused by the police.

The campaign for women's votes

In the UK, not very long ago, many people thought that women shouldn't be allowed to vote. It took until 1928 for every woman to have the same voting rights as men. There are people alive today whose grandmothers couldn't vote until then. Being able to vote was a political change. How did it come about? Was it because the men in Parliament just got together and said, 'Hey, why don't we give women the vote?'

Or was it because there was a long and hard-fought campaign for women to win the right to vote? It was indeed the latter, and in that campaign, some women lost their lives.

One of the many marches of the suffragettes, campaigning for women to have the vote.

There is also a wider question: when we look back on the campaigns, can we say that they were part of a much wider area of politics that is still being fought out today? For example, the fight for the vote campaign asked what does it mean to say that women and men should be equal? Equal meaning that they should have the same rights and opportunities. You could say, for example, that the #MeToo movement is part of that wider politics.

What's more, the push for women to vote can be traced back to campaigns going back hundreds of years for freedom of religion and universal suffrage. For example, at the end of the eighteenth century, men produced articles and laws outlining 'The Rights of Man'. Some women in France and England (like Olympe de Gouges) produced articles on the 'The Rights of Women'. That was over a hundred years before there were equal voting rights.

Spartacus

You probably know that Roman society was based on slavery. Slaves were – and sadly, still are – people who have no rights. They can be bought and sold in the same way that you can buy a chair.

In 71 BCE, some slaves in Capua, a city in Italy, were being used as gladiators to fight each other to the death for people to watch for entertainment in a stadium. A man called Appian, writing about this 230 years later said, "Spartacus persuaded about 70 of his comrades to strike for their own freedom rather than

A statue of Spartacus

for the amusement of spectators. They overcame the guards and fled."

This revolt grew into a huge uprising of some 70,000 slaves, and, although they won many battles, they were finally defeated.

THINK ABOUT

How do you think Spartacus persuaded 70 of his comrades to strike for their own freedom?

What might a slave who didn't want to join in have said? How might Spartacus (or someone else) have convinced him to join in the revolt?

What does a trade union do?

Another way in which people take political action is through their trade unions. Trade unions are organisations within industries that help working people secure better wages, benefits and conditions of work. Some say this is not political, that the officers, elected officials and union members are just trying to make sure that their colleagues earn enough, and that there are decent working conditions for people. What's political about that?

It's political because it's to do with the economy and the distribution of wealth. These are huge political issues for governments. Elections are often fought over such matters. So, although it may seem as if a hundred or so people in an office are asking for, let's say, shorter working hours, there'll be a national and political view as to whether those people should or should not work for the same pay for fewer hours, and – just as important – whether those working people should or should not take the action they are taking – like going on strike or protesting.

Action for equality

In Britain, in 1968, the women who were sewing machinists making car seat covers at the Ford Motor Company, walked out on strike. The women had been told that as part of a regrading exercise, their jobs had been graded as less skilled than similar jobs done by men at the plant, and they would therefore be paid 15 per cent less than the men.

It was common practice at the time for companies to pay women less than men, regardless of the level of skill involved in the work they were doing. As the strike continued, stock of seat covers ran out and all car production stopped. Barbara Castle, the Secretary of State for Employment and Productivity, intervened, and Ford eventually agreed to increase the women's pay in two stages until it was the same as the men's.

Have a look online or watch the film *Made in Dagenham* about the Ford machinists' strike.

The Ford machinists who went on strike in 1968.

THINK ABOUT

- How was the machinists' strike political?
- Was it just about money? Or was it about 'the status of women'? Or the 'role of women'? And equality between men and women in all things?
- How did people campaign?

Find out about the longer term effects of the strike and about the Equal Pay Act of 1970.

"We were fighting for ... what we thought was our due."

Sheila Douglas

"It was because we were women and we were just paid less."

Gwen Davis

Other kinds of political action

In one sense, every time a councillor or an MP is elected, every time a government is elected, that's a political campaign that has 'worked'.

Often in history, people have thought that this kind of politics is 'not enough' or isn't 'getting results' or is 'not representing me'.

The twentieth century was full of peoples all over the world demanding independence from the countries they were being ruled by or controlled from (Britain, Spain, France etc). They wanted the same freedoms their masters had: the right to self-determination.

The twentieth century was also known for movements and campaigns for civil rights. These are your basic rights as a person, as a citizen of a country. Most countries (not Britain) have a written constitution which tells all its citizens what their rights are.

A great deal of what we call politics has involved these kinds of questions – and still does.

Martin Luther King, Jr

Nearly everyone in the world has heard of Martin Luther King, Jr. He was one of the leaders of the Civil Rights movement in the United States in the mid-1950s who demanded that African Americans have the same civil rights as white people.

In 1963, Dr King made a celebrated address (below) at the March on Washington for jobs and freedom: 'I Have a Dream'. It is an iconic example of speech-making as an element of campaigning. You can watch a film of the speech on the internet.

The Civil Rights Act of 1964 ended segregation in public places and banned employment discrimination on the basis of race, colour, religion, sex or national origin. It is considered one of the crowning legislative achievements of the civil rights movement.

Taking risks

Sometimes people find it extremely difficult and dangerous to campaign for any kind of change. For example, there used to be a whole area of the globe that was called the Soviet bloc. It ran from East Berlin all the way across the land mass that ends on the far eastern edge of Asia. Millions of people living in those many countries were unhappy or angry with their situation, and with how things were run. But because the countries were run as police states, calling for change put people's lives at risk. In the end, in one of the most dramatic and surprising moments in history, the whole system collapsed peacefully in on itself, towards the end of 1991.

Counter campaigns

There are some campaigns which, the moment they begin, attract an opposing campaign. What takes place are what are called 'demonstrations' and 'counter-demonstrations'.

This kind of thing has been going on a long time. Here are some examples:

- When Adolf Hitler's Nazi Party started to campaign in the 1920s in Germany, there were other groups (socialists, communists and trade unionists) who campaigned against them. There were two opposed views of how society should be run battling it out in elections and on the street.

- When African Americans held demonstrations to demand civil rights, the people on those demonstrations were sometimes attacked.

Where are we now?

It may be that we're coming to a time when these kinds of divisions are stronger and more frequent than ever before. Commentators often say that the 'old divisions along party lines' are no longer relevant. What they mean is that people find themselves on different sides for different issues.

The Brexit debate, with its attendant campaigns, opposing sides and divisiveness illustrates this development well. (We'll look further into division and disagreement on pages 38-39.)

When you consider how people campaign locally and nationally, sometimes along religious lines, sometimes along 'race' or ethnic lines, sometimes along 'economic' lines (like trade unions), sometimes over gender or gay rights or sexual rights, sometimes over matters like war or conditions in other countries and so on, you can see that there is plenty of scope for people to differ on one thing, but agree on another.

> "Many individuals are doing what they can. But real success can only come if there is a change in our societies and in our economics and in our politics."
>
> *Sir David Attenborough, broadcaster and natural historian*

My experience

Nimko Ali

Nimko Ali was born in what is now known as Somaliland, moving to Manchester when she was four. On a family visit to Somaliland when she was seven, Nimko underwent FGM (female genital mutilation). In 2019, Nimko received an OBE and the International Women's Rights Award for her work on preventing FGM and gender inequality. She was also the first Somali woman to stand for election to the UK Parliament.

☀ What influenced you to become a campaigner?

I grew up in an immensely privileged family. Until the age of seven I hadn't seen any oppression and my privilege kept me in a bubble. But then two things happened, the civil war in my country and FGM. These experiences made me see inequality, and changed my perceptions. For me, politics became all about peace of mind. It was the unseen code that governed everything.

For the next twenty years or so, I was conscious of being an individual in a massive ecosystem, which is how I see politics. I started to see that gender, race, faith, sexuality, education and lived experience, all affect how the ecosystem treats you.

I was searching for the contentment I'd experienced before the FGM. The ecosystem wants to fit you into categories, but I was always swimming against the tide. I'm no *one* thing – I want to be an individual with multiple layers.

FGM underlies my political activism in the UK. I felt 'othered' at a young age. I was British and living here (98 per cent of the time), but British society didn't understand FGM. For example, when I told my teacher about my FGM she just said that's what happens to girls 'like you'. Then when I was eleven, I suffered complications from the FGM and had emergency reconstructive surgery. I was in a bad way, but nurses and staff didn't understand – there was this insistence that it was a cultural issue and should be left alone.

I didn't want to be treated differently, but until your vote counts, no one cares. I was a young, black girl, not able to vote, so there was no point in supporting me. I felt I had no power. In Africa, as the eldest child and grandchild, I was listened to. But now nobody listened.

Finding my voice

When I was eleven, I started reading a lot, especially George Orwell's *1984* and *Animal Farm*. I could see that some of us see things differently. I felt vindicated – there were other people who thought as I did.

Later, I read Nadal el Saadawi, who wrote about FGM in *The Hidden Face of Eve: Women in the Arab World*. I started to believe that success would come through education and decided that I would go to university. My ultimate plan was to have a voice to say the things I wanted to say.

Why Parliament?

I decided to try to get into Parliament as it would be a platform for putting forward ideas, and I could represent the underrepresented and ignored minorities. I believe that in our democracy we must govern for all – for the minorities as well as those who have elected the MPs. And that's the way to achieve change: to make your voice heard and be effective.

> "My ultimate plan was to have a voice to say the things I wanted to say."

How FGM campaigning changed

In 2010, with Leyla Hussein, Nimko founded an organisation called Daughters of Eve to help young women and girls who have suffered FGM or are in danger of being forced to undergo it. She told us how campaigning changed in order to be more effective.

In the early days of FGM campaigning, the mistake was to focus on the community in which it occurred. But in order to be effective you have to use the political system. Getting white, privileged men to care about young black girls broke down barriers. The first Act of Parliament to outlaw FGM within the UK was passed in 1985, but it wasn't effective since it wasn't unlawful to take girls out of the country for it.

The law needed to be changed to make taking girls abroad for FGM illegal. This was much more powerful, and in 2003, as a result of a strong campaign by Efua Dorkenoo, a new Act was passed. This extended the ban on FGM to taking girls abroad, and increased the maximum penalty from five to fourteen years' imprisonment.

I was one of the cases that Efua Dorkenoo used in her campaign.

I believe that top down is what works. When it's those who are meant to be protecting you who are instead abusing you – the voices of those in power have to be mobilised.

Why does politics cause such division and disagreement?

Politics is about who we are

It's small wonder that people get angry and argue with each other. This stuff matters! Recently in Britain we've seen huge arguments across the whole country to do with whether we should or shouldn't be part of the European Union. One moment the arguments can be about difficult issues to do with trade agreements and the next they can be about how people feel emotionally (or not) about their country.

Families

Living in families is how most, though not all of us, grow up. Families come in many shapes and sizes and they don't all conform to the same line-up. We know that families don't always stick together, people separate, move away. Sometimes new people arrive: babies, partners, relations. Families are not clubs or organisations which you join because you agree with the idea behind the club. What's more, some people in a family might be very young and others very old – and all ages in between. This means that though people in families may live together, their experiences will be very different.

The world is changing

What's more, the world is changing: new technology, new climate, new policies, new kinds of culture, people from different parts of the world mixing, factories and offices closing, new ones opening up. In some places, it becomes harder to earn a living.

Anti and pro Brexit supporters.

In others, at other times, it seems easier. The buildings and streets around us are changed by governments, planners and builders.

In an ideal world

Put the three paragraphs on page 38 together and you have all the makings of some big discussions and arguments about who we are, how the world is changing, or how the world should be.

Sometimes these discussions become very bitter. People think they are not being heard or understood. They might think that they are being deliberately deceived, or they think that other people don't care enough, or care about the wrong things.

Ideally, at the very least, we should agree about HOW to talk to each other, even if we don't agree about WHAT we're talking about. Ideally, we take it in turns, we listen to what other people are saying. Ideally, we don't say that the person we disagree with is stupid. Ideally, we avoid getting distracted from WHAT we're talking about by HOW we are talking to each other.

You'll notice that the word 'ideally' was repeated there. That's because it's only too easy to do the opposite and we end up insulting each other, instead of finding out exactly where we agree and disagree.

Ground rules

You might want to set up what are called ground rules for your discussions and disagreements. It's very hard to put them in place but it's worth trying:

- Try to find a way to make sure that everyone has a fair amount of speaking time.

- Try not to interrupt each other.

- Try not to get too close to each other or wave hands and fingers in other people's faces so that they feel threatened.

- If facts are important in the argument, make sure you verify the facts – you can use your phone or computer to check.

- Sometimes, in families, the reason things get bitter is because there's something else going on! For example, an older person might feel that a younger person should 'listen and learn' from them, and just accept what they say. There might be a whole back story about someone being bossy. In situations like this, we might say, 'Well it's not really about, say, whether you should be campaigning to keep a hospital open but about something else. Sometimes it's a good idea to take time out in a big political row, if it looks as if the argument is really about something else.

- Some arguments and rows just can't be solved with everyone agreeing. For the reasons above, we sometimes just have to 'agree to differ'.

THINK ABOUT

What sort of discussions do you have in your family? With your friends?

Can you think of times when the disagreement was about the 'back story' rather than the topic?

What do you think about the ground rules?

My experience

Sir Stephen O'Brien

Sir Stephen O'Brien was born in Tanzania in East Africa, returning to England with his family. He studied law then worked in various businesses and charities. He was a Conservative Member of Parliament for sixteen years, during which time he was also International Development Minister in the 2010 Coalition Government.

⚡ How I got started in politics

I was always interested in current affairs in the UK and worldwide, keen to know what was going on, and what I thought about it. I would argue for my position in debates and conversations. The older I became the more I realised that listening (and being prepared to change your view) was as important as speaking.

Also, I believe it's a great honour and privilege to represent people in Parliament, and I thought my experience would be useful. Ultimately, I believe politics is all about people, and how we can best rub along together peacefully, freely and fairly, and to have security and hope.

⚡ Why did I want to become an MP?

If you want to try to improve people's lives, work for a safer world, and to safeguard our planet, you can either talk or do something about it. Being an MP allows you to do both: try to persuade other people of your point of view, and learn from others what are the best policies to achieve these aims.

Politics (with a big 'P') is when everyone over the age of eighteen gets the chance to vote for those who will sit in Parliament. But we're all politicians, really. If you care about things, have ideas or just want to do your own thing, then persuading others to agree with you, or to support you, is political. It's also important to listen to other people: family, friends, your local community, teachers and employers – and adapt your thinking to find the best way forward for everyone, even if you don't agree with them.

I didn't know about politics or understand it until I realised that every day, everything we think and say and do is political, especially the minute we are with someone else.

⚹ My route into Parliament

In my twenties, in the 1980s, I joined a new Party called the SDP. It was not very successful in getting MPs elected, and when that party disappeared, I looked at the others and decided to join the Conservative Party, as it was closest to what I believed was most important. I was then selected to stand in a by-election (an election between general elections). Once elected as the winner in a tight race, I took very seriously that you must represent all your constituents – those who voted for you, and those who voted against you or not at all.

⚹ What's it like for a politician's family?

Politicians are in the public eye. It's part of the job but is a challenge for the family, especially when an MP has young children. Schoolmates can be hard on those whose parents are well-known: it's tough on young people to have to 'defend' their parent. And often the spouse is the one who, living locally in the constituency, has to handle the concerns of people whilst the politician is away in Westminster. And the MP doesn't have as much time as other parents for their family. So it is tough being the family of an MP.

Politics in the United Nations

Sir Stephen went on to become Under-Secretary-General for Humanitarian Affairs and the Emergency Relief Coordinator at the United Nations, travelling the world to coordinate life-saving work in conflict zones and where there have been natural disasters. This is what he told us about politics in the UN.

In the UN, the politics is all about persuading people from every nationality to agree to raise money and to act when people's lives anywhere in the world are in danger. What you have to do is marshal the arguments in support of your idea and proposals, take the time to make your case and listen to alternative views, adapt your approach and secure a consensus or a majority to enable a decision to be made and then carried out.

"... I realised that listening (and being prepared to change your view) was as important as speaking."

Making a political speech

You've probably heard of the terrible attack that took place in Christchurch, New Zealand in March 2019. Fifty people were killed in a mosque. We should remember that the man who did that thought he was being 'political'. He published his political manifesto.

A few days later there was a demonstration in London called 'Stand up to Racism and Fascism'. Michael Rosen spoke at it. You can read some of his speech below. He says: "You'll see that I tried to make connections between things that happened to my family and why I was there on that day protesting."

Michael Rosen speaks at the 'Stand up to Racism and Fascism' demonstration in London in March 2019.

"One of the ways we use language is to persuade other people. This is very important in politics. When I spoke at this demonstration I wanted to convey quickly and clearly why I 'stand up to racism and fascism'. As with many other public speakers, I told things with a rhythm and I told a story."

Here's some of what I said (16 March, 2019)

[...]

Today's demonstration was planned months ago long before the horror and terror of Christchurch, but it is that horror and terror we come together today to try to anticipate and to prevent.

It is because we fear it and dread it that we fight against it. But what is it?

[...]

It is what the perpetrators say it is: white supremacism.

It's been around for a long, long time.

It's been used – sometimes by newspaper people

to mock, deride and condemn minorities.
It's been used – sometimes by newspaper people, to justify invading and bombing other people's countries.
It's been used by people in power to justify slavery, segregation, discrimination, persecution and genocide.

This tells me that it's dangerous to trust those in power to fight it.

Too often, the people in power have been the perpetrators themselves.
Too often, it's people in power who've won their power and kept their power by scapegoating and persecuting minorities.

[...]

It's people in power who sent vans round saying to migrants: 'Go home, or face arrest'.
It's people in power who created what they called a 'hostile environment' for migrants.
It's people in power who created the Windrush scandal.

[...]

And it was people in power in 1943 who ordered four policemen to knock on the door of my father's uncle's room at 2.30 in the morning in a little village in western France.

He had fought for France in the First World War.
He was a French citizen.
He had committed no crime,
He wasn't ever put on trial.

In a well-organised, orderly way, according to the laws of the day, he was deported to Auschwitz and never came back.

This is the kind of thing that people in power sometimes do.

This is why I wrote a warning.

[...]

It's called:
I sometimes fear...

"I sometimes fear...
...that people might think
that fascism only ever arrives in fancy dress
worn by grotesques and monsters
as played out in endless re-runs of the Nazis.

No. Not always so.
Fascism can arrive as your friend.

It can arrive saying that it will...

restore your honour,
make you feel proud,
protect your house,
give you a job,
clean up the neighbourhood,
clear out the venal and the corrupt

remind you of how great you once were,

remove anything you feel is unlike you...

It doesn't walk in saying,

"Our programme means:
militias,
mass imprisonments,
transportations,
war,
persecution ...and mass murder."
They don't say that."

"Fascism can arrive as your friend."

What do you think?

If we accept that politics is all around us, how do we take part? As you've seen, there are lots of things we can do. We can get involved in school councils or local campaigns – for example, getting rid of plastic cups in school. We can join organisations.

There have been opportunities throughout the book for you to think about the many questions raised. Here are some more things for you to look at or do.

Investigate systems of voting

Imagine a political election in your school. How will you choose your parliament?

You could:

Create political parties. Make each class a 'constituency' and send a representative to the 'assembly'. Add up which party has got the most representatives and they 'form the government'.

Or

Ignore the constituencies and have 'lists' of possible representatives. You then add up all the votes of the school together, to determine which party wins the highest percentages. The assembly is then made up according to the percentages.

Which do you think is fairer – the constituency system or the lists system? How do you choose a leader? Do you have a prime minister and/or a president? Find out how these roles are different.

Which system do you think would be the fairest – and why?

Think about political forms

Which political forms do you think would most fairly represent the voters? Why do you think this? Discuss your opinions with other people.

● What other political forms do you know of?

● UK: Are any of the current political debates in the UK affecting you? How far are the UK political forms affecting any of these debates? If you see a current problem, how would you fix it?

The media

● Do you think one person, group or a government should control the media?

● Does it matter? If you think 'yes', why and how does it matter?

● Do the media control how we think? If you think yes, how and why does this happen?

Discuss your views

Here are some ways in which you can take part in a political discussion:

Role play

With a friend, pick a topic that you know you'll disagree about.

To start with you could play a person in your family you disagree with, while your partner takes the role of someone they agree with.

Then swap over.

This kind of role play forces you to see where the other person is coming from. This may mean that you start to agree with something you used to disagree with. Or it can mean that you try harder to get your arguments together so that you can gather together better points, or more relevant facts.

New Zealand's prime minister Jacinda Ardern's speech is broadcast to mourners at the remembrance service in Christchurch for the victims of the mosque attack in March 2019 (see page 42).

> "Empathy makes me a stronger leader."
>
> *Jacinda Ardern*

Debate

In school, you can also have a debate. There are special rules on how to argue in a debate. There's a chairperson; the topic is called a motion; people take it in turns to argue about this. There are main speakers to 'propose' and 'oppose' the motion. You have speakers from the floor chosen by the chairperson. If people stray from the topic or if they're rude or interrupt, the chairperson can discipline you. You can make 'points of order' and 'points of information'. At the end you can take a vote.

'Thrash out an agreement'

Here's another way to have a discussion about a topic: see if you can 'thrash out an agreement'. This is particularly important if it's known what has to be done, but not how to do it. A lot of political decisions are made this way so it's good to get practice at this.

Make a speech

People who are involved in a campaign might be called on to make a speech to persuade others to a course of action, or to persuade them to share a point of view. Look at the speeches mentioned in the book: Martin Luther King, Jr's 'I have a dream' speech (page 34), and Michael Rosen's speech at the 'Stand up to Racism' demonstration (pages 42–43).

Michael says that he wanted to convey quickly and clearly why he 'stands up to racism and fascism', so he used rhythm and told a story. This is a bit like writing poetry. You might like to try writing a short speech on something you feel passionately about.

Reflecting on what you've read

Think about what you've read, and about the discussions you've had while reading the book.

- Did any of these ideas surprise you? If yes, why?

- What points and values best reflect your own ideas?

- Did you change your mind about anything?

- Is there an issue that you think should be in this book but isn't?

- If you decide you want to get involved in politics, you could join the youth section of an organisation such as a political party or a pressure group that campaigns for issues you are interested in. Or you could join the student council at your school.

> "What I'm asking for is hard. It's easier to be cynical; to accept that change isn't possible, and politics is hopeless, and to believe that our voices and actions don't matter. But if we give up now, then we forsake a better future."
>
> *Barack Obama, President of the United States 2009-2017*

THINK ABOUT

WHAT MATTERS TO YOU?

- Your family's security and hopes?
- Living in a community that looks out for each other?
- The planet?
- Getting a job that allows you to make a contribution?
- People around you less fortunate than you?
- Staying healthy?
- Getting a good education and striving to be as good as you can be?
- Staying true to yourself?
- Getting enough money to enjoy yourself, not depend on others and have choices?
- Justice? Freedom?
- Other people and places in the world beyond our shores?
- Peace? Preventing and stopping conflict?
- Helping people with terrible diseases or when natural disasters wreck their lives and livelihoods?

Should you sit on your hands or should you do something about the things you care about?

Sir Stephen O'Brien

Glossary

apathy / apathetic showing no interest or energy and unwilling to take action, especially over something important

Brexit referendum a vote in which people over the age of 18 in the United Kingdom were asked (in June 2016) to decide whether the UK should leave or remain in the European Union

censorship, especially by repressive governments the act of removing parts of something, such as a newspaper article, a book or a film that they do not want someone to see or hear

civil rights rights that are designed to protect individuals from unfair treatment and to receive equal treatment, free from discrimination

coalition government a government that is formed by the joining together of different political parties, usually for a limited time, because no one party had sufficient votes to form a government on their own. (In the UK in 2010, the Liberal Democrats joined the Conservative Party in this way.)

constituency an area in which people vote to elect someone to represent them

constitution the set of political principles by which a state or organisation is governed, especially in relation to the rights of the people it governs

financial return a profit on an investment – that is, getting back more money than you put in

income support money that is paid by the government in the UK to people who have no income or a very low income

picket lines a group of workers with a disagreement with their employers who protest outside a workplace to prevent other workers from going inside

rule of law a set of laws that people in a society must obey

share(s) the equal parts that the ownership of a company is divided into, and that can be bought by members of the public

tax credit an amount of money that is taken off the amount of tax you must pay

white supremacism the system that treats white people as human and people of colour as less than human; the thinking behind racism

Further Information

Some books and websites you might find interesting:

Books

The books in the *'And Other Big Questions'* series, including *What is Right and Wrong?* by Michael Rosen and Annemarie Young (Wayland)

Politics for Beginners by Alex Frith, Rosie Hore, Louie Stowell (Usborne)

Animal Farm by George Orwell (Penguin)

Everyday Sexism, and *Girl Up*, by Laura Bates (Simon and Schuster)

Noughts and Crosses by Malorie Blackman (Corgi)

The Other Side of Truth by Beverley Naidoo (Puffin)

Websites

AVAAZ (https://secure.avaaz.org) "Avaaz is a global web movement to bring people-powered politics to decision-making everywhere."

UK Parliament education website (www.parliament.uk/education) has useful information and resources.

Simple Politics (http://simplepolitics.co.uk/about) tries to "explain processes, break down arguments and go through some of the more complicated terms used."

The Citizenship Foundation (www.citizenshipfoundation.org.uk) aims to "help young people to understand the law, politics and democratic life."

openDemocracy (www.opendemocracy.net) "...seeks to challenge power and encourage democratic debate across the world."

Amnesty International (www.amnesty.org.uk) works to "protect women, men and children wherever justice, freedom, truth and dignity are denied."

Index

More titles in the
... And other big questions series

What Is Humanism?
9780750288422
(PB Edition)

What Is Feminism?
9780750298384
(PB Edition)

Who Are Refugees
and Migrants?
9780750299862
(PB Edition)

What Is Gender?
9781526300010
(PB Edition)

What Is Consent?
9781526300928
(PB Edition)

What is Right and
Wrong?
9781526304940

What Is Race?
9781526303981

What Is Masculinity?
9781526308146

What Is Mental Health?
9781526311139